Change Your Life For The Better
4 in 1 Bundle

By David A. Hunter

Copyright © 2013-2015 David A. Hunter

All Rights Reserved

No part of this book may be reproduced
in any way or by any means without the
prior written permission of the author.

HOW TO FOCUS
ACCOMPLISH YOUR GOALS BY DEVELOPING YOUR MIND

By DAVID A. HUNTER

Text Copyright © 2013 DAVID A. HUNTER

All Rights Reserved

No part of this book may be reproduced
in any way without the written
permission of the author.

Disclaimer:
The views expressed within this book are those of the author alone. The information contained within this book is based on the opinions, observations, and experiences of the author and is provided "AS-IS". No warranties of any kind are made. Neither the author nor publisher are engaged in rendering professional services of any kind. Neither the author nor publisher will assume responsibility or liability for any loss or damage related directly or indirectly to the information contained within this book.

The author has attempted to be as accurate as possible with the information contained within this book. Neither the author nor publisher will assume responsibility or liability for any errors, omissions, inconsistencies, or inaccuracies.

Intro

The ability to focus is crucial if you wish to accomplish your goals, realize your dreams, or achieve your desires.

It's easy enough for most of us to determine what we want. Our positive thoughts turn into desires, and then our desires give us the incentive to set goals as a way to achieve them. But when we actually try to accomplish our goals, many of us tend to struggle. We encounter problems, and many of these problems are related to a lack of focus.

We have so much potential, but we allow our lack of focus to get in the way. We come up with great ideas, and then we fail to follow through on them. We get excited about starting new projects, and then we give up on them.

As we lose our focus for the things that are the most important to us, our lives begin to lack meaning. We try to multitask to the point where we end up not getting anything done.

The right kind of motivation can work wonders, but it won't always be enough. If you don't maintain a laser-like focus on your goals, things will become much more difficult than they have to be. We have distractions that need to be blocked out, obstacles that need to be overcome, and deadlines that need to be met.

Our minds continue to wander all the time. When we're at work, we think about the stuff at home. When we get home, we can't seem to take our minds off of work.

We dwell on the past, anticipate the future, and try to think about the present all at the same time.

We have bills to pay, problems to fix, friends to make time for, work to do, and sleep to get. It's easy to understand why we have trouble focusing, but it's not easy to excuse.

A wandering mind is not a bad or abnormal one, but we still need to keep it under control. There is nothing wrong with a watchdog that barks when a stranger approaches, but he needs to know that it's time to stop barking after the stranger leaves.

An excessive amount of anything is rarely a good thing. A wandering mind can allow a person's imagination to expand, while a focused mind can allow a person to get things done. You need to achieve the correct balance if you wish to stay focused on your goals without turning yourself into an emotionless machine.

It's not always a good idea to completely block out the world around you though. You need to learn how to focus on your goals without losing touch with reality. We have to acknowledge the negativity that surrounds us without allowing it to prevent us from moving forward.

Whatever your goals may be, the power of focusing on them should not be underestimated. Many successful people have reaped the rewards that come along with stayed focused on their goals. Now it's your turn.

How To Become Grounded

To ensure that you stay focused on your goals, you have to make sure that you are grounded. As obstacles present themselves in your life, you will need to deal with them without allowing yourself to get too involved in the process.

Your concentration is lost as soon as you let your energy go to the wrong places.

You need to be able to accept and appreciate compliments without allowing them to inflate your ego too much. You also need to be careful not to allow negativity to suffocate you. Empathy is important, but you need to deal with bad situations without allowing them to overpower you.

We need to be in control of ourselves. You need to be centered if you wish to stay on course.

Here are some typical symptoms that you might experience when you are not grounded:

- **Defensiveness**
- **Indecisiveness**
- **Trouble sleeping**
- **Inability to accept things the way they are**
- **Overly sensitive**
- **Feeling stressed out**
- **Temporary inflated ego followed by sudden, yet frequent crashes or letdowns**
- **Tremendous frustration**

Start by weeding out the things in your life that seem to be having a negative impact on you. Bad things will continue to happen as long as you continue to remain in bad situations.

Stress doesn't just show up out of nowhere. Bad feelings don't just show up out of nowhere. But negativity never stops presenting itself to us, and when it does, it wastes our time and makes us miserable. Instead of focusing on our goals, we are forced to focus on the things that keep dragging us down.

I know that it's easier said than done, but if we all took action to weed out the things that continue to plague us, our concentration wouldn't be stolen by negativity.

Take some time to think about the things that are really holding you back, and then if it's realistic to do so, eliminate them. Even if these aren't things that you can't completely eliminate right away, try to at least take steps towards eliminating them. Sometimes, just acknowledging the things that are bothering you the most can be a big step in the right direction.

For example, you might not be able to eliminate traffic, but instead of driving, you can choose to walk to a nearby destination. You might also wish to take a less congested route, even if it means going out of your way a little bit.

If you can catch a break, take it. Whenever you have an opportunity to reduce stress, take advantage of it.

Whenever the removal of negativity is not an option, try to balance it out by doing positive things. Leave yourself plenty of time to have fun and enjoy life. Listen to uplifting music, read interesting stories, watch inspirational films, etc.

It also helps to pay attention to your breathing. There is no need to obsess over it, but take some time (or several different times) each day to practice deep breathing. Inhale for about 5-8 seconds through your nose, and then exhale for 8-10 seconds through your mouth. Repeat this process at least a few times, but don't pass out. If you can only handle inhaling or exhaling for a few seconds at a time, that's fine. The point is to breathe from your stomach, not from your chest.

Be careful not to neglect the small things in life. An inability to breathe leads to death, but how often do we really pay attention to the fact that we are still breathing? We need to express more gratitude for the smaller things in life.

An artist is able to create a masterpiece not necessarily because he had one big idea, but because he took full advantage of a lot of smaller ideas before combining them.

The idea is to embrace every minute of the day. Treat everything that you are doing with importance. Start acting as if there is no such thing as a dull moment. After all, self-fulfilling prophesies exist.

If you have read a lot of fictional books, you might have noticed that many of the authors like to get really descriptive. They go into great detail about the town where the story takes place, what color the character's clothing is, their hairstyle, their age, their full name, the weather, etc. This is because it helps center the reader's attention on the story. It helps them become more grounded.

Here are some examples of things that you can do to help you become more grounded:

- **When you are using a computer, think about the keys on the keyboard and the screen in front of you.**
- **When you are driving a car, tightly grip the steering wheel in front of you.**
- **When you open a door, look at the door knob as you turn it.**
- **When you sit on a park bench, observe the trees, grass, and sky. Don't just sit there on your phone the whole time.**
- **Perhaps most importantly, pay attention to how you feel each day. Are you tense? Agitated? If so, ask yourself why.**

Becoming grounded is not just a one-time event; it's something that needs to be practiced and maintained, but it's worth the effort.

Get into the habit of keeping your mind in the present. Stay relaxed and don't allow your emotions to get the best of you. The less you dwell on the past and future, the more focused you will become on the present.

How To Stay Calm When You Are Under Pressure

Sometimes it seems as if there is no such thing as working under normal conditions. If employees don't get their work done, they won't be able to pay their bills. If drivers don't stay focused on the road, they crash. It can feel like the end of the world for us if we lose our concentration.

It would be nice if we could pursue our goals as if we were on a private golf course the whole time. The trees would provide privacy from the distractions of the world, and everyone would quiet down as soon as it was our turn on the green.

Unfortunately, we don't always have that luxury available to us. Occasionally, we will catch a break, but more often than not, we find ourselves climbing uphill.

Instead of obsessing over the problems themselves, we need to direct our energy towards solutions. If you are clear and specific about what you are trying to accomplish, you will be more likely to stay calm while you are pursuing your goals.

To take your mind off of the problems that you are experiencing, start thinking about the things that are going well. If nothing seems to be going well in the present, take some time to reflect on some of the memories you have of the past where things have gone well. This will get your mind to remember that good things can happen, even when you are facing major obstacles.

You have to think about what has worked best for you in the past. What was fun for you? What made you productive? What inspired you? How did you accomplish your previous goals? What helped you through tough times? How did you make it this far? What brought you good results?

It's a common reaction to think about what got in your way. Many people like to direct too much of their energy on the problem itself instead of actually focusing on how they can solve it. We spend so much time discouraging ourselves from doing the wrong things, but we forget to encourage ourselves to do the right things.

Instead of complaining, just do the best you can to work through the problem. Instead of blaming ourselves or others, we need to be constructive.

For example, a lot of drivers like to honk their horns when they get cut off in traffic. But instead of directing their focus towards applying the brakes or turning the steering wheel, they simply get mad and honk their horns.

We can't always control others, but we can usually control ourselves. Honking a horn is not a guarantee that another driver will listen, but applying your brakes (assuming that they are working) is a guarantee that your car will slow down.

Instead of stressing ourselves out about the things that are out of reach, we need to concentrate on the things that are within our control.

Let's look at another example. Let's say that you are not happy about where you live right now. Instead of dwelling on how much you hate living there, start picturing your dream house. Now picture how much money you would need in order to move into that dream house. Now picture what you would have to do to make that kind of money.

Problems are negative, but solutions are positive. Choosing to focus on negativity more often than positive things has never helped anybody in the long run. Don't let negativity steal too much of your attention. Acknowledge the problem without dwelling on it for too long.

This will get your mind to switch gears by changing your self-defeating thoughts into positive ones that encourage you to take action.

If you look at your obstacles as motivation to improve your life, the negative things won't seem as bad. Instead of thinking about all of the things that went wrong, think about how you can change things that are under your control.

For example, if a close friend dies, take time each day to appreciate the life that you have.

Some things are just too horrible to forget and ignore, but that doesn't mean we can't be thankful for the things that we have. It also doesn't mean that we can't ever recover from traumatic events.

Staying positive will allow you to stay calm when you are under pressure. Keeping your goals in front of you will make you more likely to direct your energy towards solutions instead of problems.

How To Achieve Peak Performance As You Pursue Your Goals

Nobody should be expected to maintain peak performance 24/7, but we also shouldn't be suffering from frequent work-related droughts. There will be days when we just don't feel as energized as usual, but we can't afford to let weeks go by without getting anything done.

Good performance is the result of good thoughts. You have to believe that each day is worth celebrating. Recognize that each day is another chance you have to move a step closer to accomplishing your goals.

Peak performance is not necessarily the result of discipline. It's important to have a certain degree of self-discipline, but what you really need is an incentive. We can only discipline ourselves for so long without backing it up with a real desire to improve. If you are struggling to achieve peak performance, you need to remember what it's like to be passionate about what you're doing.

Do what it takes to stay motivated. Put posters on your wall, listen to success stories about other people who have already accomplished what you are trying to accomplish, etc.

Don't forget that there is a purpose for your goals, and that there is a reason why you plan on accomplishing them. The rewards of accomplishment usually outweigh the list of failures that people experience before they cross the finish line. See each goal as an important mission.

You also need to master the art of self-awareness. Different people have different times of the day when their energy levels are the highest. You need to capitalize on these times by making every minute count before your window of opportunity closes.

Start paying close attention to how you feel at different times of the day. Experiment with different sleep schedules if you can. Try going to bed earlier, getting up earlier, getting up later, etc. Not every person really needs 8 hours of sleep every night. There are some people who actually feel better after getting 6 hours of sleep per night instead of 8 hours.

Give yourself enough time to find out what time of day your peak performance hours are. You might have multiple peak performance times spread out evenly throughout the day, or you might just have one.

There are sprint runners, and then there are marathon runners. You might be better off working in short bursts with frequent breaks, or you might end up getting more work done by bracing yourself for the long run.

Some people benefit from working hard for a few hours in the morning, and then taking an afternoon nap before feeling refreshed enough to work hard again throughout the rest of the day.

It's all about how much progress ends up getting made by the end of the day. Do some experimenting, and keep track of your results each day.

Keep in mind that mental energy is not the same as physical energy. Although the mind can have a powerful influence over the body, these two things are still different from one another.

If your goals are related to fitness, you need to work out when your physical energy is the highest. If your goals are related to academics, you need to work on them whenever your mental energy is the highest.

Sometimes you might feel physically tired, but mentally sharp. There might also be times when you feel physically capable, even if you are not feeling particularly creative at the moment.

It's okay to get tired, but make sure that you are being productive. There is a fine line between short-term fatigue and exhaustion.

Short-term fatigue is something that you would experience when you work out. You do the exercises until you feel like you have had enough, and then you go home, have dinner and take it easy. Pretty soon, you feel like you are restored and back to normal again. In fact, you usually feel better than you did before you went to the gym. You feel better because you were productive without burning yourself out.

Exhaustion is experienced when you are pushed far beyond your point of peak performance. The window of opportunity closes, but many people try to push through it anyway.

We need to work hard, but we also need to work smart. Continuously forcing yourself to skip breaks to keep working will make you more likely to get sloppy.

We need to stay consistent in order to accomplish our goals, but we can't afford to burn ourselves out by pushing ourselves too far.

This has a lot to do with your mindset. If you can develop your mind to see breaks as a productivity booster, you will be less likely to stress yourself out. Breaks lead to recovery, and recovery leads to better performance.

If you choose to work longer hours, make sure that you take longer breaks.

Keep track of everything that does and does not work out for you. Write it all down if you have to. Whenever you have a very good day, memorize the details of what happened, what you did, etc.

To summarize:

- **Be passionate about what you are doing**
- **Be aware of how you feel and why you feel that way**
- **Discover and keep track of what does and does not work for you**
- **Take advantage of your window of opportunity**

Instead of dragging yourself along all day, get in touch with what works best for you, and then follow a schedule that allows you to pursue your goals with energy and enthusiasm. Self-discipline is good, but self-compassion is better.

How To Build Up Your Willpower

Now that you recognize the importance of finding your peak performance time, it's time to talk about something else.

Although you should try to center the majority of your working hours around the time of day when you are feeling your best, you can't always rely on a certain time to get things accomplished. You need to deal with the necessities of life without allowing them to interfere with your goals.

Athletes aren't allowed to set their own hours; they just show up to practice or a game whenever they are scheduled to perform. Parents might have children that need to be picked up around the same time as their peak performance time. You might get a cold that leaves you feeling under the weather for several weeks before you finally make a full recovery.

During times like these, it takes the use of pure willpower to accomplish your goals. Working outside of your peak performance zone is much more challenging, but with enough willpower, you can still get yourself to focus.

As important as it is to be compassionate towards yourself, sometimes self-compassion can be misleading. Sometimes we feel like taking a day off, but we force ourselves to get to work anyway, and then we end up having one of the most productive days of our lives.

Things aren't always as bad as they seem, and willpower can allow us to recognize that.

You have to determine which route is better for yourself in the long run. Would you rather experience short-term discomfort to achieve long-term benefits? Or would you rather sacrifice your long-term benefits for short-term satisfaction?

Ask yourself which course of action is better for you. What would you like to look back at many years from now? Would you rather see yourself sticking to your diet, or caving in to junk food? Would you rather be living in your dream house, or would you rather stay where you are?

Start incorporating some willpower exercises into your daily routine.

A good way to practice building up your willpower is to simply get up 15-30 minutes earlier than you usually do. Pick a couple of days out of the week to set your alarm for about 20 minutes earlier than what you are used to. If that's too easy, set the alarm for an hour or two earlier.

Start eating plain food without adding spices or condiments to them. When you have baked potatoes, skip the sour cream, butter, salt, and pepper.

Dedicate yourself to small projects, and don't stop working on them until they get done. Plan things out ahead of time, and make a commitment to follow through on them.

Practice being aware of your posture. Make yourself stand up straight when you feel like slouching.

Get into the habit of embracing your uncomfortable inconveniences, but don't overdo it. Willpower has much more to do with mental alertness than physical energy. You can still push yourself when you are feeling physically tired, but if you are mentally drained, it's time to take it easy.

People wouldn't understand when I told them that I felt too exhausted to do homework after being in school all day. They would say, "How can you be tired? All you did was sit there. I'm the one who has to work every day." They didn't understand that mental exhaustion can feel much worse than physical exhaustion.

If you have ever worked all day, you might have noticed that it's easier to come home to do the physical chores such as laundry, the dishes, vacuuming, etc. than it is to do the mental chores such as writing, reading, mathematics, etc.

Even when we are physically tired, we are usually able to keep moving. But when we are mentally exhausted, we are usually spent.

Developing the mind takes a lot of mental energy, and pushing yourself too far will mentally exhaust you. Nobody has an unlimited supply of willpower. It's one of those things that has to be replenished. Treat it like a workout. Get in, work hard, and then get right back out for restoration.

Be careful with what you eat, and consume calories at regular intervals throughout the day. This will prevent mental fatigue from setting in earlier than it has to.

Exercise your willpower at the right times. Don't deliberately cut down on your sleep tonight when you know that you have a demanding day ahead of you tomorrow. Don't feel bad when the unexpected happens, and you are unable to follow through with a commitment; just try again the next day.

Let's say that you plan on finishing a book on Friday, but when Friday comes around, you have something to deal with at the last minute that leaves you feeling mentally drained. Since your willpower has already been used up due to mental exhaustion, it makes sense to give it a rest.

You can also use the power of changing your perspective. For example, you might like oranges better than apples. But if a bunch of health gurus informed you about how healthy apples can be, you might have an easier time making the transition.

Try to look for the good side of the things that you don't really want to do. Failures can be used as learning experiences, adversity can make you stronger, etc.

Exercising your willpower does not mean that you should try to push yourself through mental exhaustion. You shouldn't try to push yourself through mental exhaustion, just like you shouldn't try to force yourself to work out when you have the flu. Willpower is about resisting temptation, but you shouldn't torture yourself.

Support yourself when you fail, and encourage yourself to improve next time. Always keep your eyes open for opportunities to strengthen your willpower. When you get stuck in traffic - learn to enjoy sitting there looking out the window. When you are waiting in line at a store - use that as an opportunity to develop patience.

To summarize:

- **Practice willpower exercises**
- **Don't try to work through mental exhaustion**
- **Encourage yourself**
- **Change your perspective**

There are few things that will help you reach your goals faster than willpower, but you need to remember that you can only use a certain amount of it at a time before it gets depleted. Although energy depletion is inevitable, we can still postpone it by building up our willpower. By doing the right things at the right times in the right amounts, you can maximize your potential.

How To Use Visualization To Improve Your Ability To Focus

Another way to stay focused on your goals is through the use of visualization. The good thing about visualization is that, unlike willpower, we are not limited to a certain amount of it. You can keep practicing visualization as often as you would like. In fact, we are practicing it all the time anyway; we just don't always realize it.

The trouble is that we often use visualization the wrong way. Sometimes we choose to be negative. By choosing to stay angry, we get ourselves into the habit of having a short fuse. By choosing to become helpless victims, we end up experiencing even more depressing situations in our lives.

We start to vividly see all of the negative things that have been happening. We also bring back a lot of bad memories from the past without letting them go.

If you want to accomplish your goals, you have to start removing the things that are holding you back. Self-defeating thoughts will definitely hold you back, so you need to replace them with thoughts that lead to success.

Negative thoughts can lead to negative expectations if we are not careful. As you expect negative things to happen, negative people and negative situations usually find you.

Trying to accomplish your goals before getting rid of your self-defeating thoughts is like trying to start a fire when you are under water. You need to get out of the water before you can start a fire.

You might not always be able to prevent negative things from happening, but you can even things out by visualizing positive things.

The first thing you need to do is practice acceptance. Instead of stressing yourself out about the things that are out of your control, you need to acknowledge them, admit that something unsettling happened, and then let go of whatever it was.

The next step is to begin visualizing positive things. Start rehearsing the things that you plan to accomplish. Practice being confident and at ease. Think about the things that you will do and say once you achieve success. How will things be different after you accomplish your goals?

It also helps to visualize the different steps that you will need to take in order to accomplish your goals.

For example, if your goal is to make more money, instead of simply picturing what it would be like to have a ton of money, try to visualize being truly happy with the type of work that you do. If you are happy with your job, you will be more motivated to work really hard. If you can stay motivated to work hard, you will be less likely to give up.

If your goal is to buy a house, instead of simply picturing being inside your new house, visualize talking to real estate agents, boxing up and packing your stuff, etc.

You should also express gratitude for the things that you already have. Think of some things that you really appreciate having.

Visualizing a better future does not mean that you have to be unhappy about the present. You need to be happy with where you're at now, but you also need to realize how much better things can be if you accomplish your goals.

The idea is to really slow things down so that you can think deep. Find a fairly quiet place, and then lean back and take it easy. When negative thoughts work their way into your mind, just remind yourself that things will work out in the long run. Trust yourself to find a way.

It's difficult to believe in things that we can't see, so using your imagination can steer your mind in the right direction.

Relive some good memories, and then figure out how you might be able to incorporate some of those good things into your life today.

By visualizing a better future, you can gradually change your life. By practicing gratitude, you can pursue your goals with more enthusiasm.

It's very difficult to focus on the right things when you are unhappy with your life. Create a plan, and then see yourself going through each one of the loops to accomplish it.

The mind is like a computer. You have to program it first, and then it follows your commands. Don't just visualize the finish line, visualize the marathon.

Picture each piece of the puzzle gradually falling in place. If you stay consistent with visualization, you will start to notice opportunities that you might not have noticed otherwise.

Closing

It's important to remember that nothing is going to be easy. There will be days when your motivation level is down. There will be days when you feel uncoordinated. These things are normal and expected. It doesn't mean that you are doing anything wrong.

Remember, it's important to embrace your discomfort just as often as you embrace excitement. Perceived obstacles don't have to be so bad after all.

You never know what you might find buried in the snow if you are unwilling to dig through it. The longer you wait for the snow to melt, the more opportunities you will miss.

Once you know what you need to do, don't let negative thoughts or emotions interfere with your goals. It's time to do the things that benefit you.

Capitalize on the times when your energy levels are the highest, but don't become completely dependent on those times. Get into the habit of getting something done each day, even if it's only something small.

Habits can be started through persistent practice. Get into the habit of focusing, even when it feels inconvenient. Give yourself breaks, but get right back to it after that.

Regardless of whether or not you feel valued by others, you need to keep on going. Strive to surpass your own expectations, and you'll be amazed at what can happen.

HOW TO INCREASE PRODUCTIVITY
GET MORE DONE AND STOP WASTING TIME

By DAVID A. HUNTER

Text Copyright © 2013 David A. Hunter

All Rights Reserved

No part of this book may be reproduced in any way without the written permission of the author.

Disclaimer:

The views expressed within this book are those of the author alone. The information contained within this book is based on the opinions, experiences, and observations of the author and is provided "AS-IS". No warranties of any kind are made. Neither the author nor publisher are engaged in rendering professional services of any kind. Neither the author nor publisher will assume liability or responsibility for any loss or damage related directly or indirectly to the information contained within this book.

The author has attempted to be as accurate as possible with the information contained within this book. Neither the author nor publisher will assume responsibility or liability for any errors, omissions, inconsistencies, or inaccuracies.

Are You Really Being As Productive As You Can Be?

I remember how much time I used to waste by not managing my time the way I should have. I wasn't unproductive, but I was nowhere near as productive as I could have been. I was never really taught how to be productive when I was growing up. I just knew that I was supposed to get my work done by a certain time.

There is a lot of confusion in our lives when it comes to getting things done. Different questions might race through your mind. How am I going to get all of this done? What am I going to do? Should I work longer hours? Should I not allow myself to rest until it gets done? Am I going too easy on myself? Am I going too hard on myself? Should I just forget the whole thing altogether? Why can't I stay focused?

Maximizing your productivity is probably one of the most important things that you could ever do for yourself. There is no question about whether or not being productive is a good thing. You already know that you want to get as much done as you can, while saving as much time as possible without stressing yourself out. The question is, "How do I increase my productivity, so that I can balance my work with the rest of my life?

There is not necessarily one big solution, but a series of smaller solutions that add up as you begin to apply them. When you want to increase your productivity, it makes sense to be honest with yourself about how productive you are right now. If you wanted to lose weight, you would have to be honest with yourself about how heavy you really are. You wouldn't be able to determine how much weight you needed to lose unless you knew how far overweight you were. Productivity should be evaluated in the same way. You need to know what you are dealing with in order to help yourself more effectively.

If you wanted to run a successful business, you wouldn't just say, "Okay, It's time to be more productive." You would need to figure out what your strengths and weaknesses are. You need to keep track of how much work you are getting done now in order to determine how much time is being wasted. After you determine how much time is being wasted, you can work on gradually reducing that amount of time.

Getting a large quantity of work done will not be very beneficial if the quality suffers. Take the time to evaluate not only how much work you are getting done, but how much quality work you are getting done.

Many people like to look for excuses in order to explain why they failed to get things done. Others seem to treat severe stress as a good thing. They seem to believe that exhaustion will somehow lead to productivity.

You can be certain that something is wrong when you feel stressed out without even getting anything done. It's like running around in circles. The fatigue that a person might feel can often be mistaken for productivity. You feel like you aren't getting enough things done, so you try to force yourself to do more work. The work that you are doing becomes even more unproductive because your mind is not in the right place.

Your mind has to be in the right place if you are going to be productive. There are a number of different ways that many people like to use as an indicator for how productive they are.

Here are some examples of how some people might define their productivity:

-By how much money they make

-By how many hours they work

-By the number of compliments that they receive from their supervisors

-By the amount of praise that they receive from their clients

-By the number of tasks that they complete

Did you notice a pattern there? These things are all based on gaining some sort of assurance, largely from outside factors. Some people might feel that they need a lot of money to assure themselves that they have been productive. Others might need to rely on their supervisors to assure them of their productivity.

If we are going to be as productive as we can be, we will need something more than just money or compliments to let us know that we are doing well. It will also take more than mindlessly speeding through our tasks or working long hours each day.

What Would You Like To Accomplish By Being Productive?

Being productive involves getting things done effectively. If you are going to get things done effectively, you will need to know what your goals are. It can be easier to be productive when you clearly know what it is that you are trying to accomplish. Telling yourself, "I need to get this done as soon as possible," is not going to help you to become more productive.

Deadlines are unavoidable sometimes, but you will need motivation to make sure that you get things done by the time you reach those deadlines. Without anything good to hope for, you will end up going through life like a machine.

A lot of people seem to favor productivity because they think it helps them to pay their bills. Being more productive can lead to more money in a shorter amount of time. Making more money in a shorter amount of time can make someone more likely to pay their bills on time.

It's nice to be able to easily pay off all of your bills ahead of schedule, but it's better to have something other than paying the bills to look forward to. You might find it more difficult to be productive when all you have for motivation is to pay the bills.

Think back to your early childhood. You probably had dreams of doing special things and achieving special things. Did you really picture that you only existed in the future to pay off your bills? You most likely had plans that were fun to think about and exciting goals that kept you focused on your vision. You need to take the time to restore any excitement that you might have lost over the years.

Having a fear of not being able to pay the bills on time will provide most people with the necessary motivation to make money, but it won't necessarily provide someone with enough motivation to increase their productivity. Motivation in general might help us to get the job done, but we will need the right kind of motivation if we are truly going to make substantial progress in our lives.

For example, a supervisor might yell at an employee in order to help him perform his job a little bit faster. But it won't be good for the employer in the long term when all of their best employees quit working for them because they're tired of getting yelled at all the time.

Failure becomes a more probable outcome than success when the majority of your motivation comes from overwhelming pressure and fear. How productive can you really be when you are always stressed out?

Paying the bills is a necessity just like drinking water. It doesn't really excite anyone to drink water. People drink water for survival, not for fun. That's why most of the people I have known tend to struggle with their water intake. They only drink it when they feel like they absolutely have to, even though it's good to stay hydrated all throughout the day. They drink enough water to keep themselves alive, but not enough to make themselves as healthy as they could be. They just aren't that motivated to drink water.

You are more likely to be unproductive when you have to force yourself to do something. You end up doing the absolute minimum just to get by. Paying off your bills will help you to get by, but I'm sure that you want more out of life than to simply get by.

Paying your bills is necessary, but boring. Think of some fun goals that you would like to accomplish. Is there a vacation that you have been wanting to take? Are there any plans that have been delayed due to a lack of time or money? Are there goals that have been pushed aside because you didn't believe that they could be accomplished?

As we get older, we become more focused on our many responsibilities and obligations. It's good to be a responsible, mature person, but that doesn't mean we can't still have dreams and exciting goals for the future.

Wanting to pay your bills will motivate you to show up for work, but having positive, exciting goals will motivate you to increase your productivity.

Achieving Small Goals Can Be Better Than Failing To Achieve The Bigger Ones

It's definitely important to be excited about your goals, but it's also important that you are realistic about them. Setting goals that are too far out of reach will leave you feeling frustrated and disappointed.

It's good to have a big goal that you would like to achieve one day, but staying focused on your smaller goals can lead you to the big ones. Let's say you have a big goal to save $1,000. Your smaller goal would be to save $50. You might not be motivated to save $50 because it doesn't seem like a lot of money to you. But if you keep your goal of saving $1,000 in mind, you will be motivated to save $50 because you know that it can help you to reach your bigger goal.

If you only have small goals without ever having a big goal in mind, you might not see the point in achieving the small ones. Life can get boring without having bigger plans to pursue. You really need to have big goals as well as smaller ones. Productivity isn't increased by achieving your big goals sooner; it's increased by achieving your smaller goals on a regular basis.

You don't want to take a bigger leap than you can handle. Without small goals, you might not see any type of achievement for a very long time. It can be really discouraging to feel like you aren't accomplishing anything. If your smaller goals are obtainable, you will be less likely to give up on the larger ones.

Looking at how far away you are from achieving your goals can feel overwhelming. That's why it's important to not try to do everything all at once. It's like going on a 2,000 mile road trip all by yourself. If you're the only driver, it would be very difficult to drive for the entire length of the trip without stopping to rest. Your big goal would be to reach your final destination, but your first small goal might be to drive to a restaurant for a break. Your next goal might be to stop for gasoline. The 3rd small goal might be driving to a hotel to spend the night at.

If you only set one big goal for yourself, you might feel like a failure each day that you don't achieve that goal. When you achieve your small goals regularly, it will be like achieving a piece of your big goal each time. This way you are not only accomplishing small goals, you're getting closer to your big goal as well.

Big and small goals help to balance each other out. Thinking about the benefits that achieving your big goal will bring you can keep you motivated to achieve your small goals. Looking at the progress that you have made from achieving your small goals can encourage you to keep moving towards the big goal.

The idea is to keep the big goals in mind, while not putting too much pressure on yourself to achieve them too soon. Achieving your smaller goals will make you feel like you are getting closer and closer to the big goal, so make your smaller goals a priority. See the big goal as something that you would like to accomplish, while looking at your smaller goal as something that you need to accomplish.

Sticking To Your Plans By Eliminating Distractions

Making plans is necessary if you wish to accomplish anything, and sticking to those plans will make you more productive. There are different ways of breaking plans, but distractions are probably one of the most popular reasons for not sticking to them.

There are many different tasks that we need to accomplish throughout our lives, sometimes many at once. But if we are going to get anything done the right way, we have to know where and when to set up the necessary boundaries.

Remember that a getting a large amount of work done will not be enough to consider yourself productive. If the work is not of good quality, there is no point. It might sound a bit extreme, but distractions must be seen as almost dangerous. If you are really going to be productive, you have to start seeing your goals as amazing things, while viewing the distractions as horrible things.

Don't underestimate the power of your distractions. Being distracted while you are behind the wheel of a car can cause a serious accident. Being distracted each time you are trying to sleep can lead to insomnia. A slight distraction while you are playing sports can end up costing you the game.

The areas that we are the most successful in are usually the same areas in which we have learned to fight off our distractions the most effectively. Obviously, motivation can play a large role in how good you become at blocking out distractions. That's why it's so important to really like what you are doing.

Using your imagination to fight off boredom can really help you when you are lacking motivation. I know what it's like to work at a boring job, but using my imagination to make things interesting helped me tremendously. Embrace what you are doing and try to show some enthusiasm. Pretend that you are somewhere else if you have to, but stay focused on your work.

While working out, I used to pretend that I was on a battlefield somewhere. As I stretched and loosened up at the beginning of the workout, I would pretend that I was getting ready to approach the enemy. As I did my exercises, I would pretend that each set was a different enemy. The weights themselves were like my weapons, while the sets that I did were like the opponents that I was fighting. By the time I finished my workout, I would pretend that I had won a war.

Another idea I had was to pretend that I was boxing with an imaginary heavyweight champion. Each exercise that I did would be like another round in the boxing match. I would pretend that I lost the fight if I had a bad workout. I would pretend that I won the fight when I had a good workout. My next workout would either be a pretend re-match or a new fight with a different imaginary boxer altogether.

I would use different pretend scenarios throughout the years in order to change things up and prevent boredom. Your goals should be fun, but the things that you must do in order to reach them might not always be as fun as you would like them to be. Boredom can be a distraction in itself, so it helps to use your imagination in order to achieve a better mindset. We tend to drift away from our work as we get bored with it, but being creative can help us get back into it.

You are going to have to practice self-discipline. I've noticed that many people can't even get themselves to turn off their phones when their inside a movie theater. A person might try to justify this by saying, "I leave it on in case of an emergency." You have to start treating the elimination of distractions as an emergency. Outside emergencies usually only occur on occasion, but the emergency of trying to reach your goals occurs each day.

Be honest with yourself. Does the work that you are doing really require you to use your phone or internet connection throughout your entire working day? I have known people who were able to run their own successful customer service based businesses without having to pick up the phone every single time it rang. If the call is really that important, they can leave a message, and you can get back to them right after you get your work done.

Listening or not listening to music while you are working or studying will have to be up to you, but again, you will have to be honest with yourself. Is the music helping you to get your work done or is it just another distraction?

Sometimes you might just need to make a simple adjustment to help you get your work done without having to turn off the music altogether. Try turning down the volume lower and lower until you reach the point where you can still hear the music without it being loud enough to distract you. Another slight adjustment you can make is to change the style of music that you are listening to while you are working.

There are certain types of music that can help you study better, while there are other styles of music that can give you too much physical energy. The music that works well for you when you're at the gym probably isn't the same type of music that you should be listening to when you are sitting down at a desk. Even soft music can be a distraction sometimes, so just be aware of that.

Eliminating distractions will require that we do whatever the situation calls for. Listen to music if you feel that it helps you to work more effectively. Turn off the music if it becomes a distraction. Start testing yourself by experimenting to see what works best. Keep track of how much high-quality work you are able to get done while you listen to music. The next week, try turning off the music to see if you get more or less work done.

Doing The Right Thing By Staying Focused On The Right Things

Taking the necessary steps to avoid distraction is a good start, but sometimes there will be certain distractions that just seem to be unavoidable. You can fight off the unavoidable distractions by staying really focused on the task at hand.

Staying focused is not an easy thing to do when you are being distracted. Sometimes it can even be difficult to stay focused even when there are not that many things around to distract you. Being able to stay deeply focused on something can take a lot of practice. The ability to stay focused seems to come easier to some people than it does to others, but that doesn't mean that those people were born with special "focusing skills." You can improve your focus through practice.

A good way to start out is to keep your goals in mind as often as you can. With your goals in mind, you will be more likely to focus on the things that will bring you to your goals. Keep yourself motivated by picturing the end result of all of your hard work. Realize that in order to achieve your goals later, you will need to put in the effort now. Don't keep saying, "I have plenty of time." You might have plenty of time, but why not get started now and finish ahead of schedule?

Let's say that you want to buy a new car, but you don't always enjoy having to go to work each day. If you picture having your new car, it will be easier to stay focused on working for the money to pay for your car. You can look at every workday as another step closer to having your new car. This same type of visualization can be used to pursue any goal that you might have. Some goals can take much longer than others to accomplish, but the same type of idea applies to all of them.

I used to always experience the most problems with concentration when I was doing things that I dreaded doing. Dreaded work-related situations and low productivity levels seem to fit well together. You can't expect to focus on something that you hate doing. Most people don't like to think about things that they hate, so how can you be productive when you don't even want to think about what you are doing?

You have to get into what you are doing by recognizing the importance of it. Even if you can't find any importance right away about the work that you are doing, you can still build character as you move closer to your goals by doing what is necessary to achieve them.

Focusing requires your full attention. Something extreme usually has to happen before you can give it your full attention. The thing that you are focusing on has to be extreme in some way. There has to be something exciting for you to look forward to. When you are bored with something, you will only be able to focus on the boredom itself. If you are happy about something, it will be a lot more fun to think about the possibilities your work can bring you.

You need to focus on the things that are the most beneficial for you. You need to do the right thing by doing what is best for yourself. The only time you should be thinking about the future is when you are picturing your goals being achieved. Refuse to worry about the future. The things that happen now will become your future later on, so make sure that you are giving your attention to the present.

Concentrate on one goal at a time by thinking of that one goal as a necessity. Think of the rest of your goals as things that you would like to achieve later, but not right now. Don't confuse yourself by feeling like you have to achieve all of your goals right away. Practice patience and self-discipline.

I treat concentration similar to the way that I treat sleep. If I'm in bed for longer than 45 minutes or so without falling asleep, I know that I should just get out of bed and stop wasting time staring at the ceiling. If I am working for a long period of time and I notice that I haven't been getting much done, I usually decide that it's time to step away from the work and get back to it later.

    Difficulty with concentration does not just happen when you are lacking motivation. Sometimes you need to get away from your work for a little while to allow yourself to regain the correct state of mind. You have to balance your time between work and your time away from work. In order to do this, you will need to keep track of your time, while being careful not to waste it.

Where Is Your Time Going? What Are You Dedicating Your Time To?

In order to keep track of where your time is going, you will need to pay attention to what you are dedicating it to. We don't always realize how much time is actually being wasted when we feel like we are working hard on a project.

Stress might be a sign of work, but not necessarily a sign of productive work. If you feel stressed out, you're not going to be able to think clearly. If you're not able to think clearly, you probably won't be able to use your time wisely.

There are so many things that demand our time, but it's up to us to decide which things we give our time to. You have to stop and think about the energy that you are using. It won't be enough to just think about how you are going to get things done. You have to actually get things done if you wish to be productive.

I used to spend so much time trying to be perfect by constantly thinking about how I was going to go about doing something. It's good to have a plan, but all of my energy would go into planning things out, and not taking action. I kept using the planning strategy as an excuse for not taking action. I would convince myself that I just wasn't ready to start a new project until I planned things out better. I finally realized that my time was just being wasted while I made excuses as to why I was wasting it.

I was the guy who would read too many books and articles on a certain subject without ever applying the knowledge I had attained. I would spend most of my time trying to prepare myself for things that wouldn't even happen because I lacked the initiative to make them happen. All I had was my knowledge. I had a lot of knowledge, but it wasn't being put to good use. I thought that preparation was a good excuse, so that made it easier for me to not take action.

It was like playing hockey without a hockey stick. I would just think of it as practicing my skating. You might be practicing your skating, but you won't score any goals without a hockey stick. If you keep up that type of behavior for long enough, you will lose the game.

Your heart might be in the right place by trying to improve yourself in some way, but you have to improve yourself the right way. You can't just treat your left arm if it's your right arm that needs treatment. It's good to take care of your left arm, but in this case, your right arm needs it more.

If you have top priority goals, you need to treat them like top priority goals. It's interesting to see how easily we can push our goals aside and waste our time on less significant things.

Your results will reflect what your time is being spent on. Small tasks are usually easier to complete than the more complex, but rewarding ones. Perhaps that's why there are so many people who are living unrewarding lives. We trick ourselves into believing that we are doing something meaningful while we neglect the things that are really important. We look for the route that requires the least amount of effort while refusing to acknowledge that less effort means less benefits.

Keep track of where your time is going and try not to waste it. Being in your office for 10 hours does not mean that you worked for 10 hours. Pay attention to the amount of time that you are actually putting into your work.

You need to learn how to really appreciate the value of time. Let's say you spend 8 hours a day working, 8 hours sleeping, and 8 hours doing other things. Out of those 8 hours working, only about 3 of them were productive. That basically leaves you with 21 hours a day filled with unproductive work.

Some people like to cut down on their sleep to make up for lost time, but drowsiness starts to interfere with the quality of work being done. We want to increase productivity, not decrease it. We need to stop spending so much time doing things that don't give us anything back in return.

Working hard will ensure that you get a lot of things done, but working smart will ensure that the work you get done brings you back benefits. Before you begin any type of work, ask yourself, "What kind of benefits will I receive from doing this?" Find out if there is something better that you could be doing instead. Doing meaningless chores just for the sake of staying busy is not very productive.

Remember that you will need to put extra effort into things if you want to see better results. Do things that are worth doing. Save the less significant tasks for after you have completed your important tasks. Stop giving so much priority to your smaller chores and stay focused on the major ones. Be relentless until your most important task gets done.

There Is The Right Way To Multitask, But There Is Also The Wrong Way

What if it's not always possible to stay extremely focused on just one important task at a time? What if you can't decide which one of your tasks is most important? What if you have multiple things to complete and they all happen to appear equally important to you?

Although it's usually better to stay focused on one major objective at a time, some multitasking can actually increase your productivity if it is done the right way. Multitasking must be done in a way that will not interfere with your other tasks while still giving priority to your main objective.

Sometimes there are two different tasks you have to complete that are of equal importance. Let's say you have to do the laundry and mop the floor. Both tasks are of equal importance, but it makes sense to start with the laundry. Once you get the laundry machine going, it will take care of itself. While you are waiting for the laundry machine to complete the cycle, you can mop the floor. If you mopped the floor first, you would just be sitting there doing nothing while you waited for your laundry.

Even when something is more important, it still makes sense to start out with the task that will take care of itself once you get it started. If you have to run to the store for something very important and you also have laundry to do, get the laundry machine started first.

I like to do the dishes and get the dishwasher started before I have breakfast in the morning. I figure that I've already gone at least 8 hours overnight without food, so why can't I wait another 20 minutes? Sometimes I will have a glass of juice real quick just for some energy, but I save the real meal for after I have completed my first task for the day.

Keep in mind that you shouldn't ignore any symptoms such as dizziness or exhaustion. If you feel lightheaded, or if you experience any other symptoms due to not eating enough, you should stop and consume an actual meal.

Use your best judgment, and don't push yourself to do too many things at once. Everyone is different, and some people can handle a lack of food better than others, so stay on the safe side if you are unsure about anything. Don't work long hours without food, and always stay hydrated.

The wrong way to go about multitasking is when you put too much effort into the wrong things. All of your insignificant tasks go really well, but your main objective suffers from a lack of attention. You might not feel like working on the big project, so you make excuses for yourself as to why you are not moving forward. You know that the smaller objectives are less important than your main goal, but you dread doing the thing that requires the most work.

If that happens, you need to remember why you have that major goal in the first place. Realize that you are not going to be able to buy a house or a new car if you spend most of your time doing things that won't lead you to a house or a new car.

Multitasking is not meant to keep you busy at the expense of sacrificing your major goals. Make your main goal the center of your thoughts. The less significant goals should be worked on in your spare time. It's a good idea to multitask when your main goal is not involved.

For example, your main goal might be building a house. Your minor goals might be ordinary tasks such as light cooking, vacuuming, and doing the dishes.

In this case, you should stay focused for at least a few hours on building the house without thinking about cooking or anything else. Building your house is a big goal and you need to give it the attention that it calls for.

Once you are ready to take a break from working on the house, you can start working on your smaller tasks. Now you can start multitasking because these things aren't significant enough for you to get really frustrated with if something goes slightly wrong.

You can have the dishwasher running while you vacuum and cook. By the time you are finished eating, you can put the dishes away, and then go back to working on your main objective. It's better to focus exclusively on whichever objective calls for the most attention.

You were able to take a break while having lunch, save time by doing other chores while you had the dishwasher running, and not break up your concentration by choosing to not allow the smaller tasks to interfere with your main objective.

It's better to get the minor tasks out of the way as soon as you can, and then go right back to staying focused on the big goal. If you multitask while you are working on your primary objective, you will be less likely to be happy with the end result. You don't want to have other things on your mind when you are working on the goal that you consider to be your main priority.

You won't be as concerned if your smaller tasks don't turn out as good as you hap hoped that they would turn out. You will be much more frustrated when your bigger goals don't go as well as you had hoped that they would. For this reason, it makes sense to give all of your attention to the main goal while multitasking the smaller objectives to save time. The more time you save by multitasking the smaller goals, the more time you will have to dedicate to the main one.

Deciding On The Number Of Breaks You Should Allow Yourself To Take

The amount of breaks that you need to take can widely vary from day to day. You will have certain days when you feel that you can maintain your focus for long periods of time. You will have other days when you feel like you just can't get anything done no matter how hard you try.

The days when you seem to struggle the most are usually the same days that require the most breaks. Sometimes you will need to take the day off if you feel extremely overworked.

If you feel like you can keep on working without much of a problem, then it's better to keep the momentum going for as long as you can. You must take advantage of opportunities when they present themselves. You aren't always going to feel like you have a lot of energy to use, so keep on working until you feel like you are getting really restless.

It's important to be able to tell the difference between distractions and restlessness. The inability to make up your mind about what you want to do can fall under the category of distraction. You know that you want to complete your main task, but there are other things that you want to do as well. You can still focus on your main objective, but you can just as easily focus on something else. In this case, you should keep working on your main objective because it's more important than the rest. As long as you can focus on whatever you choose to focus on, it makes sense to stick with the more important task for now.

If you feel like you are losing your concentration and you feel like you would rather be anywhere but where you currently are, it's probably time for a break. Your mind is just not into it, so don't waste time trying to make something happen that just isn't going to happen right now.

Take as many breaks as you feel that you need to take, but don't disrupt your momentum just for the sake of taking a break. If you really needed a break, you probably wouldn't be able to concentrate so well. Don't use the clock on the wall to determine your breaks. Start using your internal clock to determine when it's time to take a break.

How Long Should Your Breaks Be When You Do Decide To Take Them?

The length of your breaks should be decided by how you feel, not by what you feel obligated to do. It might not feel right to take a longer break than what you are used to, but you might end up getting 3 times the amount of work done than you usually do when you come back from your break.

You shouldn't have to force yourself to work hard as soon as the clock reaches a certain hour in the day. Hard work will happen automatically when you work after you have been refreshed. If you feel that your break was too short, you will not come back ready to work. Your breaks should be long enough to make you miss what you have been working on.

Worrying about what might happen due to your inactivity does not count as missing what you have been working on. You have to genuinely want to get back to work because you simply have the urge to continue your work.

When I enjoyed what I was doing, I felt like a few days off was plenty. When I had a job that I hated going into, an entire month did not seem like enough time off.

You must choose your options in life wisely. If you constantly find yourself struggling to work on a certain task, then something is wrong. You shouldn't have to dread reaching your goals. The benefits of achieving your goals should outweigh the obstacles that stand in between you and your goals.

Become a firm believer in rest. Recognize that adequate rest is what will enable you to get more done overall. Clear your mind from all of the negativity that has been piling up. Give yourself enough time to forget about work for a little while. Ideally, you shouldn't take a break from your work until you crave taking a break, and you shouldn't come back to your work until you desire getting back to work.

Certain desires, thoughts, and feelings are there for a reason. The mind is letting you know that it has enough of something, does not have enough of something, or has too much of something.

If you try to work beyond your limits, productivity can suffer, and so can your health. If you take more breaks than you need, you will be wasting time.

Unwanted interruptions don't count as productive breaks, but they can take up just as much time. Blocking out interruptions can be accomplished by staying focused on what really matters. Make up your mind about what is more important. Are any interruptions right now really going to help you get your work done any faster? Is the interruption more important than what you are doing right now? Is the interruption going to help you to reach your goals?

The more respect you have for your goals, the easier it will be to ignore the interruptions. Just like a dog knows who feeds him, you should know that your work is what will bring you the rewards. Your work is what will feed you, not the interruptions.

Don't be too hard on yourself by including the interruptions as your breaks. Block out the interruptions and take real breaks, not cheap ones. A real break is whatever works best for you. Walking through a park might be enough for some people, but others might need to get out of town for a few days. It depends on how much you really need and what your budget is. What really matters is that you come back refreshed and ready to get some work done.

Getting More Done Does Not Always Mean That You Need More Time

I used to want more time to complete certain projects when I knew that I wasn't going to be able to finish them. I would always think, "If only I had more time." I didn't realize that I did not have the correct mindset at the time. I shouldn't have been thinking, "If only I had more time." I should have been thinking, "If only I could find a way to get more things done."

We can't add extra hours to the day. There are 24 hours in a day and that is just the way it is. We only waste more time by complaining about the lack of time that we have.

Remember not to lose sight of the things that are truly important to you. Time does not make or break who you are as a person. How you choose to spend that time is what really counts. Whether you have a few hours or a few decades to accomplish something, you have to make every minute count.

If you can't sleep, get out of bed and do something useful. Don't waste time tossing and turning all night. If you feel really sleepy, don't waste time trying to force yourself to work.

Go with the flow and do what you can. Being productive will require that you are functioning at your best. That means you will have to do the things that allow you to function well. You have to get enough sleep, get enough food, get enough water, get enough fresh air, give yourself enough breaks, stay inspired, and keep your motivation levels high enough.

You have to think about what is best for yourself first, not what's best for payroll. Productivity is maximized when people feel like they are in the right place at the right time. You have to appreciate your work and you have to feel appreciated for the work that you are doing.

Be confident that you are doing what is best for yourself. Try to relax and go about doing things in an easy-going way. Fight off as much stress as you can by believing that everything will work out for the best. Putting a ton of pressure on yourself to meet deadlines is an ugly way of getting things done. Desperation is not a good thing.

A better way to go is to do the best that you can, but not at the expense of experiencing misery. Pay attention to the way that you feel in order to determine your next course of action. Balance everything out to allow things to fall into place.

HOW TO STOP PROCRASTINATING
START NOW AND DON'T LOOK BACK

By DAVID A. HUNTER

Text Copyright © 2013 DAVID A. HUNTER

All Rights Reserved

No part of this book may be reproduced
in any way without the written
permission of the author.

Disclaimer:
The views expressed within this book are those of the author alone. The information contained within this book is based on the opinions, experiences, and observations of the author and is provided "AS-IS". No warranties of any kind are made. Neither the author nor publisher are engaged in rendering professional services of any kind. Neither the author nor publisher will assume liability or responsibility for any loss or damage related directly or indirectly to the information contained within this book.

The author has attempted to be as accurate as possible with the information contained within this book. Neither the author nor publisher will assume responsibility or liability for any errors, omissions, inconsistencies, or inaccuracies.

Procrastination Is Probably One Of The Biggest Enemies That You Could Ever Encounter

Procrastination can be viewed as a friend or as an enemy. We might sometimes see procrastination as a helper. We might get the idea that it is just trying to keep us out of trouble. After all, why else would we get such a strong urge to not do something if the thing that we keep putting off was actually good for us in some way?

You might try to convince yourself that you are doing the right thing by not taking action. You know that you need to do something, but you're not always sure what that "something" is. You just sense that there is a problem that isn't going away by itself. That problem is procrastination.

I had always liked to think things out before I even came close to taking action. I wanted to be absolutely certain that I was doing the right thing. I would always try my best to make sure that I was doing everything the right way. I didn't want any obstacles on my path. It's like I would try to go ahead of myself in order to clear out any potential problems before I even had a chance to experience them. I hated the idea of anything going wrong. Even the possibility of something going wrong bothered me, so I would wait.

I would assume that there wouldn't be any problems to encounter as long as I had enough time to think things through. I viewed procrastination as a friend and I didn't even know what that word meant at the time. I used to always feel like I needed more time.

The truth is that all of the time in the world is not going to help us if we don't get our lives in order. We need to get our priorities straight, and we need to stop wasting time.

Sometimes we procrastinate without even realizing it. We drop certain things in favor of less important things without seeing anything wrong with that. We assume that as long as we are busy doing something, then that's all that really matters.

You want to believe that you will accomplish your goals as soon as you are ready to accomplish them. You continue to wait for something to happen, but you never really feel like you are ready to pursue your interests. We hold ourselves back when we pursue the wrong things. The wrong thing is anything that distracts you and pulls you away from your goals.

It's alright to have hobbies and other interests, but you can't give these things more attention than they deserve. Hobbies are not a good excuse for not creating a better life for yourself. It's usually the most important things in our lives that we tend to procrastinate about the most. Perhaps you are trying to be careful in order to not mess things up. Maybe it's fear of failure. It could also be a lack of motivation. You might even believe in yourself, but have a fear of success at the same time.

Whatever the reason is, procrastination usually does more harm than good. Many things do require the right type of planning, but you need to know when enough is enough. Are you really being productive with your planning? If there is no real benefit to what you are doing, you are probably just procrastinating. If what you are doing is unnecessary, you are probably just procrastinating. If what you are doing seems to be a bit excessive, you are probably just procrastinating.

If procrastination is preventing you from living your life, then it should be viewed as an enemy. If it is holding you back from doing what you were really meant to do, then it has become one of the worst enemies that you could ever encounter. Think about it. That's exactly what an enemy does. An enemy tries to prevent you from doing what you need to to. An enemy tries to stop your plans from ever happening. An enemy does whatever it can to stop you from making any progress. An enemy will try to slow you down any way that it can.

If you are constantly procrastinating, you are basically under attack. I think the first step is to see procrastination for the enemy that it really is. Once you begin to treat the problem like it is serious, you can start to take serious action to fix it. You will try harder to put an end to procrastination once you see how bad it can really be.

When I played sports and games growing up, I used to like picturing my opponent as the bad guy. I would pretend that if I didn't win, all hope would be lost. When I won, I would feel like true victory had been achieved. It worked well for me and that was just pretend.

Procrastination is very real, making it unnecessary to pretend. You are reading this book because you already know that procrastination is bad, but I want you to start picturing it like an enemy that is trying to attack you. Being casual about a problem like procrastination is not a good way to deal with it.

Stop procrastinating about recovering from procrastination. Not taking the problem seriously can lead to more procrastination. Why would you be motivated to try as hard as you can to fix a problem when you only see it as a very minor problem? Most people are usually much more likely to attack their bigger problems first. Procrastination is one of those problems that needs to be dealt with first.

Procrastination is the reason for why you're wasting your life. Procrastination is what has been keeping you from achieving better things. Nobody likes wasting their time, but not too many people understand or appreciate the true value of time. Most people still seem to view money as more important than time. They don't seem to realize that money can come and go, but lost time is not something that you can get back.

Tomorrow will bring you another day, but it will make you a day older as well.

Procrastination is a big problem that is usually made up of a number of smaller problems. The smaller problems have joined forces to create one big problem. You will need to start picking off the smaller problems one by one before you can overcome procrastination. You will need to explore these problems and deal with them individually.

There are different fears involved with procrastination. It is important that you identify each fear that you might be experiencing.

Procrastination Can Be Caused By A Fear Of Failure

Most of us don't like to fail. We like to go through life with as few obstacles as possible and just have smooth sailing all the way. Unfortunately, life is not always that easy. There will be obstacles along the way, but that doesn't mean that they can't be overcome.

Failure is only a bad thing when we refuse to learn anything useful from it. The trouble with a lot of people is that they give up without giving themselves much of a chance. They allow failure to discourage them because they see it as a bad thing. They see it as a bad thing because they refuse to see the potential to improve. They don't realize that they can actually move closer to their goals each time that they fail.

Each failure should be seen as an opportunity for improvement. You don't necessarily have to work harder each time you fail, but you do have to try something different. Success and failure are not the same, but failure can lead to success if it is acknowledged and learned from.

I used to think that successful people never failed at anything. I also used to think that if I failed at something, then I would never become successful. It took years for me to realize that successful people deal with failure all the time. The difference is that they seem to handle it better than the way I used to. I finally learned what the trick was and it changed my life quite a bit.

I should have noticed it earlier, but at least I noticed it eventually. The trick is to not allow things to bother you so much. You shouldn't be trying to not fail, you should be trying to not procrastinate. Try to have a sense of humor about failure and don't be so uptight. Stop viewing failure as such a horrible thing.

Failing at something does not always mean that you will never get a second chance. Let's say that you fail a test in school and it ends up bringing down your grade for the class. You might not get to retake the test, but you will have other tests and homework assignments in the future. Each test that you get to take during the remainder of the semester is another chance to bring up your grade.

I think the problem is that we get too specific with what we want in life. A person who develops a crush on someone else is being too specific. When they find out that their crush does not like them back, they begin to feel like a failure. They don't want to realize that there is someone much better out there for them.

You do not automatically turn into a failure when your plans fail. Life still goes on, so stop acting like it's all over. You don't have to give up on your goals just because a particular plan did not work out. Sometimes you just need to take a different path in order to reach your goals.

If you were going on a trip and you took the wrong exit on the highway, that doesn't mean that you can't reach your destination. It's no reason to call off the entire trip altogether. You might be delayed for a little while, but you can still get to where you need to be. Sometimes taking a different route is all that you need to do. You will know when you are on the right path once you begin to follow your instincts and just allow them to lead the way.

The right path isn't always going to be easy, but it will lead you to much better things. There are so many wrong turns out there to throw you off course. It's very understandable to get lost. You need to have more understanding towards yourself if you wish to break out of the fear of failure. Be patient with yourself when you fail at something and try to understand why you failed.

You no longer need to fear failure once you understand that failure doesn't have to be a bad thing. Failure can be a bad thing if you choose to see it as a bad thing, but it can also be a good thing if you just change your perspective. Failure becomes an enemy if you decide to give up when you experience it. Don't give up. Failure should not have to get twisted into a horrible thing just because others choose to be negative and give it a bad name.

We have become conditioned to see failure as something terrible because it was unacceptable in school. If we got a failing grade on one of our homework assignments, we would usually get into trouble. We would have to stay late after school was over, we would get grounded when we got home, and we would have to go to summer school if things didn't improve fast. Others had to take the entire year of school all over again the next year.

When you get a job, it doesn't take long to discover that your boss will discipline you when they decide to believe that you failed at something. You don't want to lose your job, so you start to worry about failing at the tasks that are assigned to you.

Our fear of failure seems to come from our desire to avoid trouble. Many people want to avoid trouble at all costs. You will need to learn how to handle any trouble that might come your way as a result of your failure, or as a result of anything else. Don't go out looking for trouble, but don't allow fear to hold you back from doing the things that you need to do.

School and the workplace can make failure seem extremely bad, but that doesn't mean you have to see it as bad. If you get paid $5 an hour, that doesn't mean you are worth $5 an hour. Five bucks an hour is just what your company wants to pay you.

When you get into trouble at home for getting a bad grade in school, that doesn't mean you did something horrible. Your parents probably just wanted to see you bring up your grade.

If it were up to us, we would motivate ourselves in our own way to do better and try harder. The problem is that we were not allowed to be self-motivated, self-taught, or self-reliant when we were growing up. Even if we had a better way to handle something, we were not allowed to handle it ourselves. Sometimes we are better off learning from our own mistakes, instead of always having someone dictate what we should and should not do.

It's time to walk away from the past. It's time to get rid of the idea that failure always has to be a bad thing. Failure can bring you closer to your goals if you learn from it and make the necessary adjustments to your plans.

Understanding What Perfectionism Really Does For You

It not so much a matter of what perfectionism does for you as it is a matter of what perfectionism does to you. If something is helpful in some way, that means it is being done for you. If something is harmful in some way, that means it is being done to you.

I used to struggle with perfectionism all the time. It's not a coincidence that I also struggled with procrastination while I struggled with perfectionism. I would write songs, but I wouldn't record them. If I ever did decide to record them, I wouldn't upload them to my computer. After working out for years and receiving many compliments on how I looked, I still didn't feel ready to go to the beach.

I watched everyone else do the things that they wanted to do. They didn't seem to care at all about anything other than having fun and doing what they needed to to. I began to realize that it wasn't the perfectionists that reaped the benefits. The people that put themselves out there were the ones who got results. The people that didn't seem to have a fear of failure were the ones that made progress.

As a perfectionist, you might feel like you are making progress in some way by striving for perfection. You might believe that everything will magically fall into place once you make sure that everything is perfect. For example, a perfectionist musician might believe that he will be rich and famous if he writes a perfect song. He doesn't take into consideration that there are other factors involved in fame and fortune. Trying to write a perfect song won't do any good if you don't do anything with it. Fame and fortune won't automatically show up at your house when you write a good song. Having connections, being in the right place at the right time, and being lucky have more to do with fame and fortune than writing a perfect song.

Perfectionists always try to change things for the better and they never really feel satisfied. It's not good to never feel satisfied. Perfectionism is a trap. Perfectionism leads to irritation and dissatisfaction. It's very frustrating to feel like something is never good enough.

Imagine trying to make sure that everything about your car is perfect before you allow yourself to go anywhere. You wash it, wax it, check the tire pressure, check the oil level, and inspect everything else in the car. You keep doing this until you realize that your whole life revolves around car maintenance. You never get to go anywhere because the car never leaves the garage.

It's the same thing with your life when you procrastinate. You keep your life in a garage because you never feel ready to step out into the world. You become so obsessed with having the perfect car, you never give yourself a chance to actually go for a ride. All of your energy was directed at the wrong things, so you never reach your destination.

Your life was not meant to be kept inside of a garage. Perfectionism causes us to sit still while it tricks us into believing that we are moving forward. We miss out on better things because we believe that we have to be perfect in order to achieve those things.

Do you still want to be a perfectionist? Before you answer that question, you will have to answer these questions. Do you still want to stay in the same place without making any substantial progress? Do you want to keep letting opportunities slip away from you? Do you want to continue to feel like you are always missing out on your goals?

Being a perfectionist might not be what we thought it was. Perfectionism doesn't offer as many rewards as we thought it did. Trying to be perfect all the time is not a very pleasant way to live. We have to learn as we go along. We can't just plan for everything to be perfect, and then expect it to turn out that way.

You might need to do some initial planning before you take on a new task or project, but it's easy to get stuck on the planning phase. If you were going to exercise, you would start by stretching or warming up, and then you would work out. Next, You would take a shower, and then eat dinner before going to bed and doing it all over again the next day.

Procrastination is like spending all day stretching without ever working out or doing anything else. You need to warm up first, but you can't keep skipping your workout routine in favor of warming up the whole time. There are other things to do with your life, just as there are other things to do at the gym.

The fear of making mistakes can oftentimes be more costly than the mistakes themselves. If you do make a mistake, you can deal with it when it actually happens.

Do you remember having to get a shot at the Doctor's office when you were really young? Do you recall how miserable it was to know about it ahead of time? The anticipatory anxiety was usually worse than the shot itself. It would have been nice if they could have found a way to sneak up from behind and inject me without telling me about it ahead of time, but that's not how it works.

The fear of making mistakes is similar to the fear of failure. They both lead to procrastination. The good news is that your goals don't have to be like a planned out Doctor's appointment. You don't have to dread the mistakes that you might make as you move closer to your goals. Since you don't know for sure what might happen in the future, there is no sense in dreading the mistakes that you might happen to make.

Procrastination Can Be Caused By A Fear Of Uncertainty

Another fear that can lead to procrastination is the fear of uncertainty. Many of us seem to like being able to make accurate predictions of what might happen. We want to set certain expectations, and then have those expectations met. We all have certain habits for a reason. We like to have something that we can count on.

People have T.V. guides because they want to know which shows are going to be on before they decide to turn on the T.V. They like the idea of having a specific time set up for their favorite shows. Watching the same T.V. shows, on the same channels, at the same times each day is predictable. The problem with predictability is that it can get boring.

Even pleasant surprises can be dreadful when you suffer from the fear of uncertainty. For example, a surprise birthday party is supposed to be a good thing, but you might worry about something going wrong with the surprise. If you are the one throwing the party for someone, you might spend all of your time worrying about the surprise being ruined. If it's your birthday party, you might worry about what might happen after the party is over. Different questions might run through your mind. What if they were just pretending to have a good time? What will happen if someone did not enjoy the party? What if I don't like the gifts that they give me?

There is always something to be uncertain about. You can't go through life always trying to be certain about everything. When you are trying to overcome your fear of uncertainty, it helps to picture how boring life would be if you always knew what was going to happen next. Be thankful for uncertainty, don't fear it.

Think about what you would miss out on if you were always certain about everything.

Here are some examples:

-No more surprise endings in books or movies if you are certain about how the plot will turn out

-No point in playing sports or games if you're already certain of who will win

-No point in having conversations with anyone, since you already know what they're going to say

-No point in going to a place that you haven't been to before, since you already know what it will be like

-You wouldn't be able to experience life, since you would just be going through the motions

Uncertainty is what makes things interesting. Uncertainty is what allows us to feel alive. Uncertainty should not have to be accompanied by fear. Sometimes we're not supposed to know exactly what is going to happen. We are supposed to have faith, and trust that things will work out for the best.

It's good to be certain about your goals, dreams, wishes, and what you want out of life. But you don't have to be certain about the things that will happen on the way to your goals and dreams. You should be sure of yourself and who you are as a person, but you don't have to be certain of all the details.

If your goal is to learn how to play an instrument, it doesn't matter how everything turns out. All you have to do is practice your instrument of choice, and then just watch what happens. You wouldn't need to know right now if you will become very good at it in the future. You don't need to know how easy or difficult it might be to learn a new instrument. You don't have to know whether or not you will experience success.

The important thing to be certain about is that you are doing what you love. Be certain that you are pursuing the right goals, but don't worry about the rest. Having a fear of uncertainty is a sign that you are focusing on the wrong things. Since you are thinking the wrong thoughts, you are having the wrong feelings.

If you were always absolutely certain about everything, you would feel empty inside. It would be as if you weren't even human. You probably wouldn't want to watch a movie if you knew exactly what was going to happen every step of the way, so why would you want to know what is going to happen every step of the way in your life?

You are only looking at one side of the story when you feel that you need to always be certain about everything. You are not understanding how frustrating it would be to always be able to predict exactly what was going to happen. Always knowing exactly what is going to happen in every single situation of your life sounds like more of a curse than a blessing.

Instead of fearing uncertainty, just be glad that you are going after your goals and pursuing what you believe in. Stay focused on the tasks that you need to complete and try not to think too much about all of the things that might or might not happen.

Procrastination Can Be Caused By A Fear Of Change

Whether it's a change for the better or a change for the worse, any type of changes in a person's life can feel intimidating. The fear of change is similar to the change of uncertainty. In fact, all of the fears that lead to procrastination are similar to each other. They all stop us from doing what we need to do. But the fear of uncertainty is usually due the fear of having bad things happen. The fear of change can be experienced by anyone who fears bad things or good things.

The fear of change can be brought on by bad experiences that you had in the past. You might have changed schools in the past only to realize that you missed your friends back at the other school. You might have switched jobs only to realize that your new supervisor was a very bad one.

The fear of change can also be brought on by a fear of success. A large amount of stress can follow success sometimes. If the stress was simply too much for you when you experienced success in some area of your life, you might have picked up the impression that success is a bad thing.

Getting a promotion at a high-stress job can usually feel like it's simply not worth the extra money, but that doesn't make success a bad thing. In this case, it would mean that your high-stress job was probably not for you. It's possible that you were in the wrong field. You might have been in the wrong place at the wrong time.

You are not being fair to yourself when you allow bad experiences from the past to control your future. You could be missing out on excellent opportunities as you deliberately sabotage yourself from moving on to better things.

It's important to differentiate between success and bad experiences. You need to remove the idea from your mind that bad experiences will always follow success automatically. Remind yourself each day that success is a good thing.

Success in one area is not always the same as success in another area. If success brought you bad experiences in one area of your life, it might bring you good experiences in a different area of your life. You must separate the idea of success from the idea of bad experiences. Bad experiences are not a result of success. Bad experiences come from bad situations.

Finding success does not mean that you will be free from problems. You need to keep in mind that bad experiences can happen whether you experience success or not. Good and bad experiences can happen in all kinds of different situations, so why should success receive all of the blame for the bad experiences?

Success can come along with more responsibility than you had before, but responsibility does not have to be a bad thing. If you are pursuing the goals that you are genuinely interested in, the extra responsibility will not feel like such a chore. The extra responsibility should be a privilege, and if you don't see it as a privilege, you are probably not on the right path. We are much more likely to fear success when we are chasing after the wrong things.

Did you ever have a "Snow Day" where you didn't have to go to school? Most kids saw that as a good thing. That's because they didn't really like school to begin with.

If you dreaded the idea of not being able to go to school, that was probably because school was the right choice for you. No one had to force you to go. You wanted to be there. If you absolutely loved science class, you probably wouldn't have a problem with doing an entire science project all by yourself without any help. If anything, you probably preferred to do it yourself. Since you were doing something that you wanted to do, you didn't mind going the extra mile.

When something is a painful chore to you, of course you're not going to want any extra responsibility to go along with it. Adding insult to injury is never pleasant.

Start pursuing the right things, and any responsibility that might come along with it will be a lot easier to handle.

Think About The Future In Order To Improve The Present

Although for the most part I believe that you should stay focused on the present, thinking about your future can be helpful if it's done the right way. You shouldn't worry about your future, but you should show some concern for the life that is ahead of you.

Whenever I would feel like procrastinating about something, I would picture what my future would look like if I did or did not do something. I didn't want to have to look back at the past 5 years later and say, "If only I would have done this." It's kind of like going to a reunion party. You don't want to disappoint yourself by feeling like you haven't used your time wisely over the years. You want to be able to have something to show to everybody at the reunion party. You don't want to be embarrassed.

You might not have an actual reunion party to go to in the future, but you will still have yourself to impress. There has got to be at least one time in the past that you can remember when you were forced to miss out on an opportunity or something fun due to your procrastination. Perhaps you couldn't go to your best friend's party because you failed to finish your chores on time. Maybe you had to stay in your room to do your homework while you watched all of your friends go out and have a good time.

It's important to remember that the results you see in the future will reflect the amount of work that you put forth now. You don't want to be the one who gets caught up in a blizzard because you did not build any shelter for yourself. It's so easy to procrastinate about building shelter when the weather is still nice. You just want to enjoy the nice weather and not think about anything else. You might not think about shelter until the blizzard begins, but by then it will be too late.

There are so many different scenarios to picture. Everyone has different situations to deal with, as well as different goals to achieve. Think about the things that you would like to have happen in the future and be honest with yourself as to whether or not you are really doing everything you can to make those things happen.

Don't allow the blizzard to sneak up on you. Do the work now, and then have fun later. You can still have fun in the meantime, but make sure that you are completing a substantial amount of work each day.

If you want to buy a new car, that means you will need to save money. As long as you are saving a fair amount of money each week, you are on the right track and it's only a matter of time before you reach your goal. If you are falling behind in your savings, then you need to take it up a notch.

Look at your progress and use it to define your degree of procrastination. When you are falling behind, ask yourself, "Am I really doing everything I can to make the project move forward?"

Whatever your goals or plans for the future are, don't let yourself down. You can't stop the clock from ticking, so be sure to make the most of your time.

How To Use Decisiveness To Avoid Procrastination

Being decisive is crucial if you want to stop procrastinating. You don't have to be a powerful world leader or anything like that, but you will need to be your own leader when it comes down to making your decisions. You need to have the discipline and maturity to make the right choices in your life. The right choice might not always seem like the easiest one at first, but it can end up keeping you out of a lot of trouble later on.

The trick is to picture your goals in your mind while eliminating all of the obstacles from your thoughts. Let's say that you really want to try out a new restaurant, but you're afraid that you might not like the food. Your indecisiveness causes you to procrastinate about going to the restaurant. You know that you really want to go, but you allow your fear of the unknown to paralyze you. If you stay focused on the restaurant itself while disregarding the possibility that you might not like the food, it will make more sense in your mind to just go.

You have to take fear out of the equation if you wish to be decisive. Remember, the fear itself is usually worse than actually experiencing the bad situation that you were worried about. You don't have to go back to the restaurant if you don't care for the food, but you won't know for sure until you try it out. If you were never really interested in the restaurant to begin with, then don't go. But if there is something that you know you want to try, don't let the obstacles stop you.

Eliminate all of the negative feedback that comes along with the pursuit of your goals. Obstacles are not the end of the world, but never doing the things that you need to do might mean the end of you.

Procrastination can be a really bad habit. Even when you procrastinate about the smaller things in life, it could make you more likely to procrastinate about bigger things in the future. If you are being plagued by indecision, stop allowing negativity to take over your mind. Think about all of the good possibilities while not allowing your worries to control you. If a worrisome thought enters your mind, just say, "Yeah that's a possibility, but I will handle it if and when it happens."

Conquer your negative thoughts with positive ones. Don't let the bad thoughts win. The good things that could happen usually outweigh the bad things that could happen when you are going after your goals. You need to focus only on your goals. Don't focus on the negativity that you might experience while you are working on your goals.

You will find it easier to make the right decisions when you are confident that you are doing what you believe in.

Are You Keeping Track Of Time Without Wasting It?

We don't always realize how much time we are wasting when we are on our own. Sometimes we need someone else to help put things in perspective for us.

I used to go about each day feeling like I got a lot done. I would work out, practice playing my guitar, do some chores, and then cook dinner. One day my friend came over just to see how I was doing. He stuck around for a while and talked to me as I did the laundry and stuff like that. There was something about him being there that made me realize how much time I was allowing to pass me by.

The same thing would happen when I was working out at the gym. When I worked out at home, I found it easier to take my time and have a less productive workout session, but at the gym with other gym members all around me, I felt more motivated to work out harder. I realized that I had more energy than I thought I had. I was able to exercise at a faster pace than what I thought I was capable of. I discovered that I was able to work out more productively when I was under pressure. If anyone was watching me when I worked out, I considered that to be pressure.

It felt like the same thing when my friend stopped by for a visit. When I was doing chores, I felt like I should work faster if I had someone watching me. We need to learn how to watch ourselves in order to make sure that we are not wasting time.

There isn't always going to be someone there with you, so you need to catch yourself when you are being unproductive. Don't be too hard on yourself, but be firm enough to place yourself back on the right path after you have wandered off.

It won't be enough to simply keep track of time. You have to make sure that you are using your time to your fullest potential. We don't have anyone to judge us when we are working on something all by ourselves. If you procrastinate in front of someone, they will think that something is wrong.

If you count your money at home, you will be more likely to take your time doing so. But if you were counting money as a cashier in a store, you would probably want to go fast in order to keep the line moving.

Sometimes we don't realize our own strength until our strength is tested. We understand that we have deadlines to meet, but we choose to procrastinate anyway. But as we push ourselves a bit harder, we realize that we can do more.

Pretend that you are monitoring yourself. Would you like what you saw? Would you hire yourself? Does it look like you are really putting effort into what you are doing? Does it look like you are wasting time?

You wouldn't procrastinate if you knew that someone was there watching, so why should you procrastinate when you know that you are there to watch yourself?

When you feel like procrastinating about something, pretend that you have an entire audience watching and counting on you to complete your task. Treat whatever it is that you have to do like an important mission. Once you begin to give your responsibilities the priority that they deserve, you can move forward without looking back.

How To Keep Your Momentum Going Without Looking Back

Breaking through the barrier of procrastination is one thing, but you will also need to keep a steady pace once you get started.

If you have trouble keeping the momentum going once you get started on something, you can start as small as you want, and then just work your way up from there. If you get the urge to stop what you are working on after 5 minutes, try increasing that time to 7 minutes next time. Continue to increase the amount of time with each session. The progress might seem slow, but it will be steady and solid.

There were plenty of times in the past where I would try to set a small amount of time for myself to work on something that I didn't feel like doing. I would promise myself that I only had to work on it for a short time, and no longer than that.

What I noticed is that once I got myself going on the task I dreaded, I found it almost difficult to stop. The trick is to relieve the pressure that you might be experiencing. If you give yourself the idea that you have to totally commit yourself to something without giving yourself any breaks until it's done, you'll end up talking yourself out of it altogether.

If someone offered you a bundle of merchandise for an expensive price without even letting you sample any of it, would you want to buy it? But if someone offered something for a very low price and allowed you to sample it first, you would probably be more likely to buy it.

It's not that the high-priced bundle of merchandise wasn't any good. The idea is to have as few strings attached as possible. You don't have to make or sign any contracts with yourself. The only agreement you have to make with yourself is to get started and stop procrastinating. Basically, you don't have to promise yourself that you will cross the finish line, but you do need to participate in the race.

Once you remove this unnecessary and counterproductive pressure from the picture, you will be more likely to just keep on going. Looking back is something you do when you are unsure of something. But why would you feel unsure of anything when there is no pressure involved?

It's usually the pressure that keeps us from doing the things that we want to do. We have to eliminate this pressure by freeing ourselves from the commitments that intimidate and prevent us from moving forward.

Major commitments can come later, but for now, the only thing you have to commit to is getting started. Working on a dreaded task for a few minutes a day is still an improvement from never working on it at all.

Remember, it's usually the anticipation of the dreaded event that seems to overwhelm us more than the event itself. Some days will be more difficult than others, but if you keep increasing the amount of time spent on a task, while eliminating the pressure to be perfect, you will find more of a reason to keep the momentum going, and less of a reason to look back.

HOW TO ACHIEVE SUCCESS
TAKE CHARGE OF YOUR DESTINATION IN LIFE

By DAVID A. HUNTER

Text Copyright © 2013 DAVID A. HUNTER

All Rights Reserved

No part of this book may be reproduced
in any way without the written
permission of the author.

Disclaimer:

The views expressed within this book are those of the author alone. The information contained within this book is based on the opinions, observations, and experiences of the author and is provided "AS-IS". No warranties of any kind are made. Neither the author nor publisher are engaged in rendering professional services of any kind. Neither the author nor publisher will assume responsibility or liability for any loss or damage related directly or indirectly to the information contained within this book.

The author has attempted to be as accurate as possible with the information contained within this book. Neither the author nor publisher will assume responsibility or liability for any errors, omissions, inconsistencies, or inaccuracies.

Beginning Your Journey On The Path That Leads To Success

Even though failure gives us a chance to improve, success is what we ultimately desire. Many of us are only willing to fail if we believe that our failures will lead to something much better later on.

Everyone has different goals in life, but we need to understand that success for one person might not feel like success at all to another person. A high-paying career will not make someone feel successful if that person is feeling trapped inside of a high-stress, dead-end job. Having a really nice house will not make someone feel successful if that person is lonely and unhappy. The end of one person's journey might just be the beginning of another person's journey.

It was years before I found out what I really wanted in life. The things that sound good right now might not sound as good to you later on. Our goals might change over the years, but the root of our desire stays the same. We need to know and understand what the root of our desire is.

If you don't know what the root of your desire is, your feeling of success will always depend on superficial things. There is nothing wrong with having a desire for a lot of money, but you need to have a good reason for having a lot of money. Would you use your money to help others, or would you keep it all to yourself? Would you be responsible with all of your money? Would you be able to add more value to the world if you were rich?

Even if you feel like you are absolutely certain of what you want, take some additional time to think about it. It's good to have an idea of what you want, but you must also know why you want the things that you hope to have.

Before you can experience success, you need to realize that you have choices. Even if you become really good at something, you might have difficulty feeling successful if you were forced into doing it. Success comes from achieving the things that we want in life, not the things that we don't want. It doesn't always feel like we have choices, but we do. We have choices, and if we choose to be unsuccessful, we only have ourselves to blame.

We usually feel unsuccessful when we refuse to take charge. We have the choice to take charge of our destination in life, but when we feel like we are unable to move forward, we start to believe that we have no choices.

In order to achieve true success, you have to enjoy the journey itself. If you feel like you are unable to move forward, this is because you are not enjoying your journey. Even though the journey is filled with obstacles, you can still have fun along the way. If you are hating every minute of your journey, you are probably on the wrong path. Life does not have to be miserable just because you are trying to succeed.

Do you remember being forced to read a lot of boring material in school that you had absolutely no interest in? When that happens, a lot of people will try to tell you that you "don't like to read." But when you find a subject that you are interested in, you find yourself reading all the time. That's what you need to keep in mind when you are looking for success. You need to pursue the things that you are interested in.

All of the good things in life seem to stand along the same line.

Here are some things that can make you feel successful:

- **Good health**
- **Peace**

- **Happiness**
- **Prosperity**

Achieving one of these things can open up the door for opportunities in other areas. These things are like different branches on the same tree.

For example, prosperity alone might not be enough to make you feel successful, but it can lead to a sense of accomplishment. A sense of accomplishment can lead to increased confidence, and then confidence can lead to peace and happiness. Peace and happiness can lead to good health.

Success isn't necessarily defined by just one thing, but you can use that single thing as a steppingstone for other good things. It's easier when you have something to work with.

Success requires hard work, but the work should not burn you out. Success requires discipline, but you shouldn't have to feel like a robot.

Short-term success is nice, but long-term success is what really counts, and if you want to experience long-term success, you will have to get used to experiencing short-term failure. It's better to learn from your mistakes now, and then succeed later than it is to have a little bit of success now, and then watch it all fade away. Short-cuts can be tempting, but it's better to have solid, long-term success.

The journey to success might not be easy, but since when is it fun to do something easy? Is it fun to play a game when you know that you will easily win every single time? Life is more interesting with challenges. We just need to make sure that the challenges in life do not overwhelm us. We need to see the challenges as good things that are waiting to happen.

How To Adjust Your Attitude To Invite Success Into Your Life

A positive attitude is a good start, but it will take more than that to achieve success. Many people can be affected by another person's attitude, but no one can affect your attitude more than yourself. If we were truly happy, we wouldn't allow another person's bad attitude to have such an impact on us. We blame others for putting us in a bad mood when we don't want to admit that we are not as happy about our own lives as we would like to be.

When we learn how to let go, we put ourselves in a position of power. We give ourselves the power to be happy and control our own lives. So instead of just having a positive attitude, we will also have power, and that's the combination we are looking for. Our positive beliefs have to be more powerful than the negativity that we encounter.

Refusing to stay depressed, refusing to stay discouraged when we face rejection, staying calm under high-stress situations, and refusing to give up when things get difficult will give us power. We lose power when we make bad choices. A bad attitude does not have to be an automatic reaction to the negative situations in your life. We need to process and filter the negativity without losing control of our emotions.

Think about how you can replace your negative thoughts and feelings. Without being forceful, try to encourage the situation to make the transition from negative to positive. Even if you can't always turn everything into something positive, you can always make the situation less horrible than it appears to be.

It's alright to hate a bad situation, but you shouldn't allow the bad situation to control you. When you compare the place you are at right now to where you would like to be, it can leave you feeling depressed and discouraged. It's better to accept where you're at now before admitting that you want more out of life.

Feeling bad about failing isn't always a bad thing. Feeling bad about failure is an indication that your hunger for success is still alive. Giving up after you experience failure is an indication that your hunger for success is dead. Keep your hunger for success alive by remembering what you really want.

So here are some points to focus on:

- **Positive attitude**
- **Power**
- **Self-control**
- **Positive belief**
- **Self-awareness**

No one really likes a bad attitude. Let's say that you are a manager, and you had the choice between hiring someone with an impressive resume, but a bad attitude, and someone with less experience, but who also has a lot of potential. Who would you rather hire? It makes sense to go with the person who has a desire for improvement.

No one wants to work with someone who acts like they know everything. There is always something else to learn, but not everyone is willing to listen. Arrogance is pushy, rigid and condescending, but confidence is polite, flexible, and understanding. Having a solid belief in your own abilities while leaving yourself some room for improvement shows confidence. Even with less experience, the confident person with the right attitude will succeed in the long term.

The trouble is that a lot of people are not even aware of their negative attitude, but that doesn't have to be you. Monitor your thoughts carefully, and if you notice yourself being negative, steer yourself back in the right direction.

People aren't going to care what your background is. Even if you have a really good reason for being upset, people are going to want to keep their distance if you handle your emotions the wrong way. You can choose to have a bad attitude, but don't be surprised when you end up attracting a lot of people into your life who have bad attitudes as well.

There are different ways of looking at a situation. A negative person will choose the absolute worst possible route, and then run as fast as they can toward it while trying to convince other negative people to follow them.

If you want true success, you will need to have the ability to draw the right people into your life. Let's say that you have a lot of money, but a bad attitude. You will end up attracting people that just want to use you for your money. Attitude counts. Your attitude can eventually determine your whole lifestyle. It's better to have one real friend than it is to have a countless number of people who are only interested in using you.

Whether it is intentional or not, there will be people who steer you in the opposite direction of success. You need to learn how to identify the wrong types of people who will try to manipulate you. These people can come in the form of complainers, narcissists who only pretend to care about you, overly charming sociopaths who only want to use you, etc. If you are sure about what you want, don't allow anyone to talk you out of it.

Everyone likes to stay focused on seeking the approval of others, but they don't understand that their own thoughts about themselves are what's really the most important. It's certainly not a bad thing to have some support and encouragement from others, but if you really want success, you are going to have to learn how to believe in yourself when no one else does. You should always make an effort to surround yourself with people who bring out the best in you, but the idea is to learn how to bring out the best in yourself without being dependent on others doing it for you.

You can bring out the best in yourself by:

- **Being kind to yourself and others**
- **Giving yourself a chance by believing in your abilities**
- **Being confident**
- **Enjoying life and having fun**
- **Taking care of your health**
- **Being optimistic**

Going through tough times is no excuse to be a pessimist. Being happy doesn't mean that you simply wait for things to change. You can start improving your life right now with a good attitude.

How To Build Character And Develop Integrity

Your confidence and overall chances of having success can really improve when you actually stand for something. It's always much easier to stand up for something when you strongly believe in it.

The reason why so many businesses and relationships fail is because they lack integrity. Failed businesses and bad relationship partners have high expectations for their partners and employees, but they fail to give anything good back in return. They fail to give anything back because they have no integrity. They are selfish and greedy.

There are other people who do the right things, but for the wrong reasons. It's not enough to simply do the right thing. You need to understand why it's so important to do the right thing. If fear is the only motivator you have for doing the right thing, you will never be able to build up your integrity to its fullest potential.

Little kids understand discipline. They understand that they will be in trouble if they get caught doing something that their parents told them not to do. But it's difficult for them to build character if they don't even realize that they did anything wrong.

You shouldn't have to discipline yourself. Discipline is forceful, and it's difficult to achieve any type of success when you have to force yourself to do something that you don't really want to do. The idea is to have a genuine desire for doing what's best for yourself and others. For example, I remember that the students who did the best in school were the same ones who actually wanted to spend hours on their homework each day. Their parents didn't have to tell them to do well in school. Since the burning desire was there, they didn't need a coach or boss to discipline them.

School is just one example. No matter what your goals are, you will need to learn how to do things because you want to do them, not because you feel like you have to. Start looking for the benefits in every situation. For example, if you don't like to eat vegetables, remind yourself that since they are healthy, they might prevent you from getting sick. Your thoughts have to be in alignment with your actions. If you don't believe in what you are doing, you are wasting your time.

When you are confronted with major conflict, you are going to need a strong foundation to stand on. Your foundation cannot be strong unless you are able to maintain your moral principles.

Building character and integrity involves different things that all take time and practice to develop. You can try to do a little bit of everything all at once, or you can pick one thing at a time to focus on entirely.

Here are some of the main qualities that are involved in building character and integrity:

- **Accepting responsibility for the choices that you make**
- **Being trustworthy**
- **Bravery**
- **Honesty**
- **Self-respect**
- **Empathy**

Although our environment can really have an impact on our integrity, who we choose to become is up to us. Being raised in a bad environment can have a negative impact on our integrity, but we can break bad habits just like we can recover from an injury. Some injuries take longer than others to recover from, but recovery is possible. We can start fixing our bad habits by replacing them with good ones.

Let's start with responsibility. It can be challenging to truly appreciate what responsibility really is at a very young age. Kids get allowance money after they complete their chores, but it's difficult for them to see anything beyond that. Since they want their allowance, they do their chores. It can take years before we realize that responsibility has more to offer than allowance money.

By complaining about what others have done, we shift the responsibility over to them. By shifting the responsibility over to someone else, we actually give up our power. When people feel powerless to change their situation, they usually end up complaining even more, and then the whole thing just becomes a reinforcing cycle of hopelessness and misery.

You shouldn't beat yourself up over a negative situation, but you need to claim responsibility for the things that you have allowed into your life.

These things can include:

- **Grudges**
- **Bitterness**
- **Self-hatred**
- **An unwillingness to listen**

We don't have to control the things that happen to us, but we need to control our thoughts about them.

Let's say that you encounter someone who is being offensive in some way. It would be wise for you to try to avoid this person, but it would be unwise for you to hold a grudge against them. It's not necessarily your fault that you encountered the offender, but only you can make the decision about whether or not you should remain bitter about the situation from that point on.

It's more about claiming responsibility of your thoughts, emotions, and actions than it is about claiming responsibility of things that are outside of your control. If you choose to stop associating with an offender, it's the offender's loss. If you choose to never trust anyone again, it becomes a great loss for you.

Bitterness can eventually lead to self-hatred. Many people will try to project the blame in an outward fashion, but they will eventually realize that they are only lying to themselves. This can lead to self-destructive behavior. Habits can turn inward just as easily as they can turn outward. The kinder you are to others, the kinder you will be to yourself. Try to walk away from negativity as often as you can.

Be willing to listen to your intuition. It's good to listen to helpful advice from others, but ultimately, you will need to listen to your own intuition. Good advice from others will guide you in the right direction, but the final decision rests on your instincts.

Being honest can lead to trustworthiness over a period of time. It might not always feel as if they have many instant rewards, but they certainly pay off in the long run. It's easier to achieve success when people have confidence in you. Being reliable and trustworthy will make others feel at ease when they are working with you. Whether you wish to be successful with work or relationships, honesty and trustworthiness are crucial.

Since others will always be expecting you to live up to your expectations, being trustworthy can involve a great deal of responsibility, and more responsibility means more work. But just like with anything else in life, we have to be willing to endure the additional workload that comes along with the benefits. If we want the benefits, we will have to work for them.

In order to allow others to trust you, it's important that you learn how to trust yourself. In order to trust yourself, you have to be sure of what you want, be sure of what is right, and be sure of what you are trying to accomplish. Once your values are in order, you need to trust your intuition. You need to earn your own trust before you can truly earn the trust of others.

Dishonesty is a sign of insecurity. If you want to achieve success, you will need to be honest with yourself. You need to acknowledge your weaknesses so that you can work on improving them. If you are comfortable with who you are, you shouldn't have a problem being honest with yourself. Making mistakes does not make someone a bad person. It's difficult to grow without making mistakes, and you won't be able to learn from your mistakes if you're not honest with yourself about them.

As you look for success, it's also important to have empathy. If you strongly dislike something, chances are that plenty of other people will dislike it as well. Although different people have different likes and dislikes, there are usually some common similarities that most people share.

For example, most people:

- **Dislike bullies**
- **Dislike harassment**
- **Dislike rudeness**
- **Dislike being unappreciated**
- **Dislike bad attitudes**

That's just a basic starting point, but once you are able to identify the things that you don't want, you will be able to work on any character flaws that are bringing you the things that you don't want. The better you understand yourself, the better you will be able to relate to others and improve your life.

If we want success, we need to attract positive things in our lives. If we want to attract positive things in our lives, we need to have empathy. If employers wish to be successful, they will need empathy in order to relate to their employees. If teachers wish to be successful, they will need to empathize with what their students are feeling. If parents wish to be successful, they will need to empathize with what their children are feeling. Successful relationships require both sides to have an ability to understand and experience the same types of feelings.

Different situations will require different approaches. You need to have the appropriate behavior for every situation. Sometimes people want attention, but sometimes they want to be left alone. Some people might want you to have a conversation with them, but others might just want you to acknowledge them by smiling. Developing empathy will help you understand what to do in each unique situation.

You can't effectively comfort someone if you don't understand what they are going through. You also can't have a good conversation with someone if you don't know how to relate to them. Although ruthlessness and bullying might lead to a promotion, wise managers understand that they will hurt themselves in the long run if they resort to such tactics. What good is a promotion if it doesn't lead to true success?

We need to show a genuine interest in other people's lives if we wish to empathize with what they are feeling. Many people might say the opposite of what their feelings really are, but you can usually pick up some clues by reading their body language. Actions can usually speak for themselves, and if you read them correctly, you might find the truth.

We also need to encourage the right people in the right way. For example, Instead of trying to force introverts to socialize, try to encourage them (in a subtle way) to interact with other people. Encouraging others in a polite way will not only bring out the best in them, it will bring out the best in yourself as well.

Having character and integrity will also require bravery. The key to bravery is to think about all of the good things that you will miss out on if you choose to let fear get the best of you. Instead of dreading obstacles, be thankful for opportunities. Fear can be exciting if it's kept under control. For example, roller coasters can be intimidating initially, but if you can work through that fear, you can end up having a lot of fun.

Fear doesn't have to be so bad if you look at it the right way. Sometimes fear is rational, and sometimes it isn't. Disregard the irrational fear, and embrace the rational fear. Being afraid of your boss is an irrational fear. Getting fired and not having any money is a rational fear, but being afraid of the boss himself is irrational.

The rational fear can actually help you. Not only does it keep you out of danger, it can also encourage you to make some scary, yet necessary changes in your life. Being afraid of your boss won't help you, but being afraid of poverty can prevent you from getting lazy.

It's never a good thing to live a life that's full of fear, but when it's experienced in small doses, it can give you that extra bit of energy that you need to move forward in life. Use fear to your advantage and be brave enough to stay positive as you face negativity.

How To Work Hard Without Stressing Yourself Out

Success is achieved through hard work, but stressing yourself out can kill creativity and overall productivity. Hard work has its benefits, but it also has some drawbacks. One of those drawbacks is stress. Since stress is not going to leave us alone when we are trying to get a lot of work done, we need to find a way to deal with it.

There is a difference between stress and being stressed out. Being stressed out is something that you wan to avoid at all costs, but an occasional small amount of stress is usually unavoidable when you are working hard.

You need to monitor your stress level to make sure that it doesn't cross the line.

You will need to observe your:

- **Mood**
- **Level of motivation**
- **Level of happiness**
- **Level of satisfaction**

If you started a project with enthusiasm and excitement, and now you feel depressed, tired and unmotivated, you have probably allowed stress to get the best of you.

The trick is to enjoy the journey as you progress toward your goals. We set goals for ourselves that take years to accomplish, and when we fail to make the kind of progress that we were hoping for, we end up pushing ourselves too far.

There will be times when pushing yourself is necessary, but demanding more out of yourself than you can handle is not the answer. We need to find balance. You need to know how much is too much, and how much is not enough.

Working out can put us under tremendous physical stress, but it can also relieve us of mental stress. Unless the person has a medical problem, the physical aspect of the stress from the workout would be a small price to pay compared to the mental benefits that it produces.

Doing something that is intellectually challenging can also be a good form of stress. Although it takes a generous amount of mental energy to solve a mathematical equation, there is a good feeling of accomplishment that is achieved after the problem is solved.

The feeling of being stressed out falls upon us when we do too many of the things that we absolutely hate doing. Even if you liked what you were doing initially, there might be certain negative aspects about your job, task, or project that have overwhelmed you. We need to handle these negative aspects by giving ourselves enough time to recover from them.

If you are in a situation that you don't want to be in, give yourself enough time to remind yourself that it doesn't have to be this way forever. When you are in a positive situation, remind yourself that your hard work is what made it possible. Allow the good things to encourage you, and allow the negative things to motivate you to do better. Thinking like this will allow you to win either way.

The things that we enjoy doing might bring us some stress, but it usually doesn't feel like stress. When we spend a lot of time doing the things that we love, we might feel mentally stimulated, but not stressed out.

Feeling stressed out is an indication that what you are doing is no longer fun. Instead of experiencing encouragement, we experience discipline, and instead of feeling productive, we feel exhausted.

Success requires focus, but it also requires rest and a chance to get away from everything. You need to give yourself a break each time you feel like you have had enough. Depending on the type of work you are doing, a break could be anywhere from 5 minutes to 3 days or longer. Ideally, the shorter the break, the better, but make sure that it's long enough to allow you to be as productive as you can be once you get back to work.

Doing good might be more important than feeling good, but that doesn't mean we can't make happiness one of our top priorities. We need to be happy with what we are doing, and then we need to sharpen our skills. Many people do this backwards. First, they pick a job that is not right for them. Then, they try to force themselves to get better at a job that will hopefully make them happy one day. We do the same thing with relationships. We settle for the first person that comes along, and then we try to turn them into something that suits us. What we really need to do is work on improving ourselves first, and then patiently wait for the right person.

We can be stressed out at a bad job that we are very skilled at, and we can be stressed out at our dream job if we lack the necessary skills to go along with it. You need to know what makes you happy before you start to sharpen your skills, just like you need to know what you are building before you develop a blueprint. You will handle stress a lot easier when you are confident that whatever it is you are doing will eventually lead you to happiness.

Sometimes you need to ask for help when you are really struggling with something that you really want to do. Just because you can't get something done right now, that doesn't mean it can't get done at all. Outsourcing might be a good choice for you if you simply feel like you need help with a project.

If you want to handle stress, you will need to have control over your emotions. Stop settling for less. Stop rushing into the wrong relationships because you are afraid of being single. Stop trying to force the wrong things to happen.

When our effort is directed the wrong way, we will feel stressed out. We put all of our effort into getting more work done at all costs. If we direct our effort toward happiness, motivation, and positive encouragement, our hard work will flow naturally. As we regain our inspiration, we become much more productive.

Short-term success is achieved through hard work and discipline, but long-term success is achieved through hard work that flows easily as we enjoy what we are doing. It all comes down to getting your priorities straight.

The top priorities are:

- **Enjoying life**
- **Enjoying your work**
- **Believing strongly in what you do**
- **Health**

The idea is to make the work flow naturally by being in the right state of mind. You have to stop forcing yourself to do the wrong things at the wrong times.

That doesn't mean you should sit around for weeks at a time while you wait for inspiration to come to you. This is a process that might not take shape right away. In the meantime you still have to work, but make sure that you are always leaving yourself enough time to work on your mindset as well. Some days will be more challenging than others, but you still have to try.

As you gradually make the transition toward a better mindset, you will find yourself getting more done in a shorter period of time without stressing yourself out.

How To Fight Your Way Through Apathy

By now you should understand the importance of controlling your emotions, but what if you feel like most of your emotions are gone? It's difficult to control our emotions when we are feeling numb and indifferent towards life.

Apathy should not be mistaken for boredom or laziness. Apathy can be similar to stress in the sense that it can kill your creativity and productivity. But apathy does not mean that you are uncreative or unproductive.

You can fight your way through apathy by:

- **Realizing that you have a purpose in life**
- **Finding that purpose**
- **Setting goals to help you fulfill that purpose**
- **Taking small steps towards achieving your goals**

There is almost always some kind of trigger that sets off our apathy. We need to find and identify it. Think back to when you first started noticing the symptoms of apathy. Even when there is not a specific event to inject us with apathy, we can usually remember some type of negative thinking pattern that brought us here. Have you been trying to control things that are out of your reach? Have you been setting yourself up for disappointment? Have you been convincing yourself that there's no point to your goals?

The important thing to remember is that your goals won't just disappear because you are feeling apathetic. Your goals are just sitting on the sidelines waiting for you to pick up the pace again. You don't have to do everything all at once. You can start off as small as you want, but you have to start somewhere. Sometimes you just need to take the first step, and then the momentum becomes self-sustaining, even if you didn't want to do whatever it was initially.

We are creative, even when we are feeling apathetic. If we weren't creative, we wouldn't be able to come up with so many new excuses as to why we can't motivate ourselves to do the things that we need to do. We just need to transform that negative creativity into positive creativity.

You might feel as if you have no desires, but you do have them. They just need to be reignited. Apathy is not where you want to be, so picture yourself where you would like to be. That should give you an idea of what your desires are. Picture what you might have to do to get to where you would like to be. Oftentimes, the things that we keep resisting are the same things that we need to do the most.

Commitments can be intimidating when you are experiencing apathy. Although you have to start something, you don't have to finish everything. Feel free to try something without having to commit to it right away. Even when it's difficult, sometimes you just have to push yourself to get started without pushing yourself too hard.

One of the reasons we experience apathy is because we don't believe that there are any rewards for what we are doing. We need to remember that our persistence will eventually pay off. You need to remember that there is a reason to be productive. Even after you accomplish one goal, there are still reasons for accomplishing many other goals. There are amazing plans with your name on them that are just waiting to be fulfilled. Each day is another opportunity for growth, will you accept it?

Take Charge Of Your Journey By Being In Control

If you want to achieve success, you will need to realize that you are in control of your ultimate long-term success. We might not be able to control all of the things that happen on our journey, but we certainly have control over our ultimate destination. That's what makes it fun. We know where we are going, but we still have surprises along the way.

Put yourself on the pathway that leads to good things. Get enough rest, consume a healthy diet, and try to resist temptation. Doing these things will allow you to think clearly. We become what we do, and we will achieve success as long as we are able to focus on the right things and use our energy for the right purposes.

Your journey in life is not out of control when you can't see what's ahead of you. Your journey in life is out of control when you don't feel compelled to move forward. We might have a desire to reach our goals, but we need to resist the desire to give in to the things that take us away from our goals. We need to stop causing conflict in our lives.

Focus on one major goal at a time, and when you fail, try again. Focus on the things that bring you long-term value, not short-term satisfaction. Don't be afraid to think about changing your values if the ones you currently have are not bringing you the results that you desire. Maybe wealth is not as important to you as you thought it was, or maybe you are starting to realize that it's more important to you than you would like to admit. Once your values are in order, you will be able to make better decisions.

Hold yourself accountable for the amount of success that you have in your life, and you will have control of your journey.

www.ingramcontent.com/pod-product-compliance
Lightning Source LLC
Chambersburg PA
CBHW081249180526
45170CB00007B/2356